Deaf <u>Tend</u> Your

A Guide to Mouth Morphemes in American Sign Language

Deaf <u>Tend</u> Your

Also by Dr. Byron Bridges Published by Winkshop

Native Fingerspelling

Classifiers

Topography

Linguistics of ASL 101

Dr. Byron Bridges and Dr. Melanie Metzger

Deaf <u>Tend</u> Your
A Guide to Mouth Morphemes in
American Sign Language

Co-Authored and Co-Directed by Dr. Byron Bridges

and

Co-Authored by Dr. Melanie Metzger

DVD content Co-Directed and Produced by Wink

Published by Winkshop, Inc
2015

Deaf Tend Your

First Printing: 2015

ISBN 978-0-9856760-2-5

Winkshop, Inc
1600 Maryland Ave
#312
Washington D.C. 20002

www.WinkshopASL.com

Special discounts are available on bulk purchases by corporations, associations, educators, and others. For details, contact the publisher
Contact@WinkshopASL.com

U.S. trade bookstores and wholesalers: Please contact the publisher:
Contact@WinkshopASL.com

Dedication

We would like to dedicate this book to the memory of Stephen M. Ryan. Steve was a cherished friend, well-loved by everyone. Passionately involved in the instruction of American Sign Language, he was considered a true ally and teacher, as well as a supporter of Gallaudet University. In an effort to increase public knowledge and awareness of American Sign Language (ASL), the Deaf community, and Deaf culture, he conducted many workshop presentations, comedy performances, and brainstorming sessions on related topics.

Steve was involved with the research of the first version of this book from the beginning, and unselfishly contributed his time, heart, and love to this project. With his untimely death, the Deaf community and the field of sign language instruction lost a dear friend. He will always be sorely missed.

Contents

Acknowledgements

First, I want to thank the Deaf Community directly. I respect, value, and love our language and culture. It is my hope that *DEAF TEND YOUR* will have a positive impact on your life. I also hope that more and more people will learn sign language including mouth morphemes, thereby increasing communication access within families, workplaces, schools, and the communities where you live.

Although there are not enough pages to express my gratitude to each and every person who has crossed my path, it is important that I mention a few names specifically. It is with such joy that I thank those who first welcomed me into the Deaf Community, who taught me their beautiful and rich language and culture, my mother and father. Margie Lee and Lloyd Wayne, from the bottom of my heart I thank both of you. I would not be where I am today if it were not for you. I would also like to thank my sister, Dr. Bobbie Beth Scoggins, who has always made the best out of me. I love you, Bobbie.

I'd also like to acknowledge the educators and mentors who have guided, mentored, and encouraged me on my academic and professional journey. Thanks to the late Edmund Booth, the late Sam Lane Sr., Danny McClurkan, Fred Gobel, the late Stephen Ryan, Dr. Jean Andrew, Dr. Melanie Metzger, Mel Carter, Mickie Burton (who agreed to be a model in our video examples), Rebecca Reihm, and every person who believed in me. It is instructors and mentors like you whom I strive to emulate.

Thank you to Winkshop for continually pushing to get this product finished. A book like this one will open so many doors for people to learn American Sign Language. It is my sincere goal that this textbook increases mainstream knowledge of American Sign Language and Deaf culture. Thank you to Wink Smith and my son, Jesse Harris for working so hard to make this project a success.

To my kids, Kizzie, Brandon, Jesse, Dylan, Cassidy, Tyler and Haley: You all mean the world to me. Every one of you are different in your own ways. I am glad you are part of my life. I wouldn't want it any other way. Love all of you equally.

I would like to thank my ASL family (AAAD, NBAD, ASK DR BYRON on Facebook, fishing folks). Your constant ASL signs

Deaf <u>Tend</u> Your

and creativity help me follow my dreams wherever they may lead, and this has never gone unrecognized. A special thank you to Dr. Melanie Metzger who co-authored this book and made this possible.

Finally, I would like to thank you, the person holding this book. Thank you for taking the time to learn American Sign Language. By taking this step, you have the ability to make a Deaf person's day brighter through your desire to communicate using their language.

– Dr. Byron Bridges, 2014

Glossing is used to transcribe linguistic symbols of one language using the writing system of another language.

For this text, ASL phrases are presented in video form, accompanied by a glossed transcription and an English translation. Note that glossed transcriptions will include gestures and non-manual information only as relevant to the discussion. Other gestures and non-manual information will not be transcribed, in order to simplify the transcription for the reader.

The glossed examples in this text follow these guidelines:

SIGN
  gloss of a manual sign or mouth morpheme
#WORD
  gloss of a lexicalized fingerspelled word
L-E-T-T-E-R-S
  gloss of a fingerspelled word
SIGN++
  gloss of a sign repetition
CL:
  gloss of a classifier predicate
  (followed by letter/number indicating handshape)
subject-VERB-object
  gloss of a verb that includes subject/object referents
(action)
  gloss of visual/spatial/contextual information
  nms
SIGN
  gloss of a relevant non-manual feature
SIGN
  gloss of a sign with an ASL mouth morpheme
IX
  gloss of lexical pointing (indexing)

After working with many American Sign Language (ASL) classes, it became clear that something was missing. The lessons lacked information about parts of language not expressed by the hands: non-manual information. The likely reason most classes have not included more about the non-manual aspects of ASL is that there has been relatively little research on this subject and few resources available for use by ASL teachers. This book, *DEAF TEND YOUR*, is designed to provide this information.

It is necessary to begin with a discussion of the definition of ASL. Fortunately, an increasing number of researchers are devoting attention to this topic because it is essential to define ASL before acquiring it and teaching it correctly to others. So, what is ASL? Many different definitions currently exist and few people have come to complete agreement on one clear and standardized definition of it. Whether one considers ASL to be the language of native signers born and raised by Deaf ASL users, or to be the language of anyone who uses signing as a primary language, in our opinion the following is clear: ASL includes facial expressions, head movements, and body movements. These are known as non-manual signals (NMS). NMS are important because through the use of these signals, an observer can recognize fluency in ASL, just as a person native to France or Germany can recognize a native speaker of his/her own language through pronunciation, rhythm and stress, not only through vocabulary and grammar.

Deaf individuals come from a variety of backgrounds and not all Deaf people are native ASL users. There are ways of discovering native ASL users. The process of identifying native ASL users is relatively simple; they are generally those who use the mouth and tongue movements which will be discussed in detail here. This information can be very important to students of ASL who are interested in socializing with native ASL users to immerse themselves in the language. Thus, one purpose of this book is to assist in the identification of ASL, which in turn, will help facilitate development of the appropriate use of NMS. This book offers a window; perhaps the view will entice you to immerse yourself in ASL. Learning non-manual signals is the door to becoming fluent in the language. However, be forewarned: once the door has been opened, most people never go back through. Because of that, ASL and the Deaf community become lifelong friends.

ASL is a rich language and NMS are only one small part of it; the ASL structure includes phonology, morphology, and syntax. While under the study of morphology (indivisible units of meaning), NMS can alter the syntactic (sentence-level) meaning. Examples of such influence will be addressed throughout this book. One aspect of NMS, as discussed here, focuses on the use of the face. To this end, the face may be divided into four parts: eyebrows, eyes, cheeks, and mouth.

We will spend most of our time on mouth morphemes, which are non-manual signals on the mouth. Our research shows that the mouth generates a variety of adjectival and adverbial information in ASL, including options for intonation. By comparison, English speakers can alter the meaning of a sentence using vocal intonation:

EXAMPLE: *This* is your pen.
This *is* your pen.
This is *your* pen?
This is your *pen.*

There is a tremendous amount to learn about the use of mouth morphemes in ASL, and much research remains to be done. It is our hope that this book will serve as a catalyst, spurring additional research and curricula on this important topic. Our purpose here is to give students of ASL the opportunity to know what to look for with regard to NMS; to be able to observe and identify various forms of NMS, and learn how to use them in the future.

The importance of NMS in ASL has led us to design *Deaf Tend Your* for two groups: students of ASL who are second language learners (for example: teachers, interpreters, and students) and native ASL users who are formally studying their language – much like native English speakers taking English courses. For those who are second language learners, the study of NMS should prove to be quite valuable, especially for those employed as professionals working with

Deaf people. For example, deaf education teachers who are skilled in using NMS and evaluating their appropriate use will be a rare, yet essential, commodity in any bilingual-bicultural educational program. Parents interested in gaining greater fluency in ASL to improve communication with their deaf children will also find this information helpful. Interpreters and students of interpreting are in a better position to facilitate communication with ASL users by having a deeper knowledge of NMS. As video relay service (VRS) interpreters have replaced telephone relay operators, the use of NMS plays a more significant role than ever in communication between Deaf and hearing audiences.

The authors of this book reflect the same diverse backgrounds as its intended audience. One author is Deaf, a native user of ASL, an interpreter, and a linguist. The other is hearing, learned ASL as a second language, and is also an interpreter and a linguist. Thus, this book reflects both a linguistic view of the structure of ASL, as well as second language learner and native perspectives. It focuses on the use of NMS in ASL for second language learners, native language users studying ASL structure, interpreters, teachers, and others seeking proficiency in ASL. The English text is supplemented by videos including valuable examples and exercises.

The text is arranged in the following format: Chapter One discusses the importance of NMS to ASL users, and provides information regarding past research on NMS in ASL. It includes a discussion of constructed action, conversation regulators, and facial expressions that represent emotions. Chapter Two addresses NMS as grammatical markers. Chapter Three focuses specifically on mouth morphemes in ASL and the procedures used to obtain information about mouth morphemes for this book. Lexicalized mouth morphemes are discussed in Chapter Four, and mouth morpheme modifiers are addressed in Chapter Five. Chapter Six and Seven continues with examples of ASL mouth morphemes providing examples of sentences where they might occur. Chapters 1-7 include a set of review exercises. Chapter Eight is a summary of the previous chapters.

Whether you are a new student of ASL, an experienced interpreter looking brushing up on your skills, or a native signer interested in the complexities of your language, we hope this book

Deaf Tend Your

will help you expand your knowledge. Join us on this journey as we uncover the oft-overlooked world of NMS – we know you will never look at ASL from the same perspective.

– BB & MM

Note to the reader:
This text will follow standard academic conventions with regard to writing "Deaf" and "deaf."

"Deaf" will refer to identification with the sociocultural Deaf community; "deaf" will refer to physiological hearing loss.

Chapter 1 Non-Manual Signals in ASL

For many years, no formal recognition existed of the importance of non-manual linguistic features in signed languages. It was not until the work of William C. Stokoe that people even realized American Sign Language was a structured linguistic system. In 1965, Stokoe, with Dorothy Casterline and Carl Croneberg, published the first dictionary of American Sign Language (ASL) based on linguistic principles. This dictionary demonstrated that signs, like the words of spoken languages, consist of meaningful parts. In spoken languages, words are built from small units of sound which are produced at a certain location in the mouth (with the tongue near the teeth, for example), in a specific manner (with air moving in a continuous stream, with an "explosion" of air, and so forth), and either with or without the voice. These building blocks, grouped as consonants and vowels, are combined in a series of syllables to form words and sentences.

The signs used in signed languages such as ASL are also built from small units. These units are visual and spatial and consist of handshape, location, movement, palm orientation, and non-manual signals. These visual-spatial units are combined in a series of movements and holds to build meaningful signs (Liddell & Johnson, 1989). Over the past 50 years, linguistic researchers have discovered much about the structure of ASL. This structure is composed of the same three linguistic categories that outline the study of any language: phonology, morphology, and syntax.

The study of the units that are combined to create meaningful words/signs within a language is referred to as phonology. ASL phonology deals with the building blocks that form signs, and how they are assembled into those signs. For example, manual signs are made up of hand configurations (handshape) at certain places around the body (location) with the hands facing in a specific direction (palm orientation). These parts are combined in a series of movements and holds (movement), to create meaningful utterances.

To illustrate, the signs for TRAIN and SHORTLY (see figure 1.1) use the same handshapes, location, and movement, but differ in palm orientation. Similarly, the signs for SUMMER, UGLY, and DRY (see figure 1.2) differ only in location but share common handshape, orientation, and movement.

> **Please refer to the DVD for:**
> **Figure 1.1 TRAIN and SHORTLY**
> **Figure 1.2 SUMMER, UGLY, and DRY**

Morphology focuses on meaningful utterances. Morphemes in ASL are those signs or processes which have meanings associated with them. For instance, if one were to sign the verb glossed as WAIT, the sign has an indivisible meaning associated with it and is, therefore, one example of a morpheme in ASL. If one were to add a circular movement while signing the verb WAIT, such that the hands repeatedly move in a circular motion (up and away from the body then down and toward the body) the process of this motion adds another meaning that can be translated into English as, "for a long time" (Klima & Bellugi, 1979). The meaning associated with this movement remains constant even when accompanied by different ASL verbs. Thus, it is an example of a process morpheme in ASL. Morphology also relates to how new words are formed in a language through processes such as compounding. RED-HAIR, FEEL-LIKE, and FEEL-NOTHING are all examples of compounds in ASL. The role of mouth morphemes within ASL morphology is an area which warrants further research.

Syntax refers to the rules that govern formation of grammatical sentences in a language. NMS that function as grammatical markers are especially relevant to syntax. This topic will be addressed in Chapter Two, when discussing the essential role NMS play in forming the grammatical structure of certain sentence types, such as yes-no questions and wh-questions.

Early ASL research focused a lot of attention on the use of the hands. However, in the 1970s, researchers began to examine not only what the hands do while one is signing ASL, but also the meaning of non-manual signals such as facial expression and head and body movement (Friedman, 1975, 1976; Kegl & Wilbur, 1976; Baker & Padden, 1978; Liddell, 1977, 1980; Baker & Cokely, 1980).

The discovery non-manual signals and their usage in ASL has proven significant in many ways. Researchers have found that non-manual signals function as modifiers (comparable to adverbs), and they function grammatically in distinguishing certain clause structures as well. It has also been found that non-manual signals are able to serve as a form of visual intonation, parallel in some ways to intonation carried by vocal pitch in spoken languages. Moreover, as Wilbur (1987) points out, non-manual signals can consist of many different parts. These parts, which include the eyebrows, cheeks, mouth, and so forth, can signal different pieces of information all at one time. Since research on NMS is relatively new, further research will likely demonstrate additional important aspects of NMS.

Currently, enough information is known about NMS to indicate that the study of this aspect of ASL is crucial to both first and second language learners. Often, Deaf people are able to identify native speakers of ASL by the signer's appropriate use of NMS. For second language learners, gaining fluency in ASL may be dependent on their ability to use NMS appropriately. Further, it is essential that individuals be immersed within native ASL environments if they are interested in ASL fluency.

Many non-fluent students of ASL believe that all deaf people are native ASL users, but this is not the case. Prior to the recognition of ASL as a language in the 1960s, educators of deaf children felt that these children needed to learn spoken English to become educated. Yet, since deaf children could not hear spoken English, educators devised numerous ways of attempting to provide access to the English language. One such strategy is oral/aural education in which deaf children are taught to read lips and use any residual hearing they might have. Another strategy involves signing some of the vocabulary of ASL (or variations of these signs) in English word order to try to represent English via signs (Signed English, SEE 1, SEE 2, LOVE, etc.), while mouthing the English words. Historically, the only Deaf children who had consistent exposure to ASL as a first language were those who had grown up in Deaf families, or at residential schools with other Deaf children of Deaf families. Today, deaf people are a large and diverse group of language users. Some deaf people are native ASL users, others may use some form of English-like signing. Still, some deaf people do not sign at all.

A further complication occurs when deaf and hearing people come in contact with one another. When one is native in ASL and the other is native in English, a unique form of signing often results. Once thought to be a form of pidgin (Pidgin Signed English, or PSE) (Woodward, 1973), subsequent studies by Ceil Lucas and Clayton Valli (1989, 1991, 1992) indicate that the result is actually a form of contact signing that incorporates some features of both languages. A study by Jeffrey Davis (1989) examined the use of ASL with English-like mouthing, for example. Given the numerous varieties of signing a student of ASL might run into, an understanding and recognition of NMS can help to distinguish ASL from other types of signing. Thus, one purpose for studying NMS is to assist in the identification of ASL to facilitate language development.

The next section will address previous findings on the functions of NMS in ASL. Subsequent chapters will describe various types of ASL mouth morphemes based on recent research (Bridges, 1993). Nevertheless, the recognition and understanding of non-manual signals is a critical aspect of learning ASL.

Non-manual Signals

Non-manual signals refer in general to those aspects of ASL that do not involve the use of the hands, and are an integral part of ASL. There are at least six known types of NMS: reflections of emotional states, aspects of constructed action, conversation regulators, lexical mouth morphemes, grammatical markers, and modifiers such as adverbs. Each of these types has a different function in ASL. The role of lexical mouth morphemes, grammatical markers, and modifiers will be addressed in later chapters. The remainder of this chapter will focus on NMS as representing a signer's feelings, constructing actions of characters from narratives, and regulating conversational discourse.

Universal Expressions of Emotion

In many cultures it is well known, although not always consciously, that a person's feelings can be observed in his or her face. When someone is surprised, angry, or happy, these feelings can often be seen reflected in the person's facial expressions. Liddell (1980) points out that more than 100 years ago, Darwin suggested that these facial expressions are universal. Research published by Ekman & Friesan (1975) supports Darwin's claim. They found that some facial expressions, such as that for surprise – which includes a dropped jaw and wide eyes – are consistent in form throughout many different cultures. The situations in which expressions are used, of course, will differ among different groups of people with varied values and customs.

Because facial expressions that express certain emotions appear to be universal, it seems logical that these same facial expressions will be used to reflect the feelings of signers. Liddell's (1980) research supports the expectation that facial expression can reflect the feelings of the signer. In addition, the research distinguishes these NMS from the facial expressions that occur within an ASL sentence. They can be associated with the speaker, the subject, or even a particular sign. For example, the facial expression for sadness will probably occur when a signer signs SAD, whether the signer feels sad or not. However, when the signer signs the following with a sad expression, the expression reflects the signer's personal feelings:

<u>brows raise</u> <u>sad</u>
MY DOG   DIE **(Figure 1.3)**

> **Please refer to the DVD for:**
> **Figure 1.3 MY DOG DIE**

Liddell suggests that the use of facial expression to reflect a signer's emotions in ASL can be compared to the use of vocal intonation to convey a speaker's feelings within a spoken English utterance. Thus, an English sentence such as: "My dog died," could be spoken in a way that indicates whether the speaker is feeling shocked, saddened or relieved. Native English speakers also often display facial expressions that reflect their feelings of sorrow, surprise, unhappiness, amusement, and so on.

Signers can also convey the emotions of others. In ASL, one way of expressing what other people have felt, said, or done is through what has historically been referred to as role-playing, role-shifting, or perspective shifting. In such an instance, a signer might identify an upcoming action or quote as belonging to a specific person, akin to the English speaker tag, "Mary said..." As Liddell points out, when a signer quotes or represents the actions of another character, the use of facial expression can reflect the feelings of that other person (in this case, Mary). This occurrence introduces another function of facial expressions and other non-manual signals within ASL, which brings us to the next section.

Constructed Action

Constructed action (Winston, 1991; Metzger, 1995) refers to a way in which ASL signers convey information about other people and places. Traditionally referred to as role-shifting, constructed action is a way of representing the actions and dialogue of others. It can include not only gesturing and signing their words, but also directing their eye gaze as that character, and moving the body to distinguish certain mannerisms. For example, when a signer tells a story about a child talking to an adult, the signer would look up to where that adult would be from the child's point of view. Constructed actions and dialogue, also called performatives (Winston, 1991, 1992), have been described as a form of pantomime. McNeil (1992) describes a distinction between gestures, pantomime, and signs based on the work of Adam Kendon (1988). Kendon describes gestures as spontaneous hand or arm movements that are made while a person is speaking. An example of this would be when someone is moving their arm in circles while saying in English, "…and the slide at the playground went around and around…"

Pantomime, on the other hand, refers specifically to the use of the hands, body, head, and face to represent specific objects or actions. For instance, Liddell (1980) describes a pantomime in which a signer signs "PENNY MAN," then reaches into his pocket and pulls out his hand such that the fingers seem to have a penny between them. Next the signer puts his hand behind his shoulder and appears to drop the penny behind his back. Only the signs PENNY and MAN are actual signs. The rest of the signer's actions are a form of pantomime, according to Liddell (1980). While pantomime is a form of communication not limited to any particular language, this aspect of ASL has received increased attention among researchers in recent years. Some have discussed the NMS involved in constructing the actions and dialogue of characters within stories and lectures (Lentz, 1986; Padden, 1986; Roy, 1989; Engberg-Pedersen, 1992; Winston, 1991, 1992, 1993; Bridges, 1993; Liddell, 1995; Metzger, 1995).

Constructed action is not limited to narratives or human characters. Roy (1989) discusses the constructed actions and dialogue of the fish in an ASL lecture. The types of non-manual signals involved in constructed actions are extensive and include eye gaze and facial expressions, as well as head and body movements.

Conversation Regulators

When two or more people are engaged in a conversation, they unconsciously use culturally shared techniques that determine who talks when and how they take turns within the conversation. Mastery of these conversation regulators will prevent second language learners from seeming rude by inadvertently using inappropriate eye gaze. Baker (1976), Baker & Padden (1978), and Wilbur & Petitto (1983) address some of the techniques used by signers to regulate conversations in ASL; these techniques are a form of NMS.

Baker notes that eye gaze is frequently used to regulate who has the floor during an ASL exchange. Essentially, a signer in conversation has the option whether to make eye contact or not. A signer generally makes eye contact to begin a turn, and can then look away while signing. One of the reasons the signer will make eye contact again is to allow someone else to have a turn in the conversation.

Eye gaze has also been found to be a regulator for classroom conversations. Mather (1989) found that native Deaf ASL users seem to use eye gaze as an effective technique for managing classroom interactions. Mather also found that with young deaf children, the use of individual eye contact with each student helped the teacher to maintain control of the class. In contrast, gazing around at the entire group of students tended to result in confused or even chaotic interactions. In addition, Mather found that when a teacher signed a question to two or more students without making clear eye contact to one individual, the students were confused about who was expected to answer. In this manner, the use of eye contact can be seen to function as an important regulator of classroom interaction.

Future work will likely provide greater insights into conversation regulators including the use of eye gaze. For example, it seems likely that there are rules that govern the direction of eye gaze; side-to-side gazes seem to be natural in conversation, whereas gazes up and down seem to carry additional meaning. Eye gaze plays an important role within NMS, contributing to multiple aspects of the language. It has been shown to be an important technique for regulating conversations in a variety of situations. Based on the findings regarding eye gaze, it is clear that appropriate use of NMS to regulate conversation can help students of ASL respect cultural norms within the Deaf community.

Chapter One Review

1. Whose work helped people to realize that American Sign Language is an organized and structured linguistic system?
2. Are all deaf people native ASL signers? Why or why not?
3. To what does the term non-manual signal (or NMS) refer?
4. List three functions carried out by non-manual signals.
5. Describe one type of non-manual behavior that is possibly universal and one that is language-specific.
6. Create a sentence in ASL that involves at least one NMS which reflects an emotional state within constructed action.

Dr. Byron Bridges and Dr. Melanie Metzger

Chapter 2: Non-Manual Signals as Grammatical Markers

Many grammatical markers in ASL involve the use of non-manual signals. Even in initial research regarding ASL, the fact that non-manual signals could serve grammatical functions was clear. For example, Stokoe (1960) recognized that side-to-side head shaking could indicate negation even when no manual sign was present to support such an interpretation. Grammatical NMS also include eyebrow movements, which can distinguish one type of sentence from another. Although some debate on the matter still exists, research has shown the basic sentence structure of ASL to be subject-verb-object (SVO) order (Fischer, 1975; Friedman, 1976; Baker & Cokely, 1980; Liddell, 1980). However, this is only one of several sentence structures available to ASL signers. In many languages, including both ASL and English, a thought can be expressed using a variety of sentence structures. The two ASL sentences: "ME ARRIVE HOME SOON" and "SOON ME ARRIVE HOME" are both grammatical and have basically the same meaning. Likewise, English grammar allows both of the following to have roughly the same meaning: "I will leave for the store at 4 P.M." and "At 4 P.M. I will leave for the store."

Certain grammatical structures can help separate statements from questions. NMS are often used to distinguish questions from statements, and to separate different types of statements. This subject has received a fair amount of attention. When NMS distinguish questions and statement types they are called grammatical markers. Research on grammatical markers has revealed that NMS are involved in many aspects of ASL grammar, including topicalization, relative clauses, conditionals, yes-no questions, wh-questions, rhetorical questions, and negation.

Topicalization

One option signers have when expressing themselves is to state the topic and then comment about it. This is called topicalization. The topic-comment structure involves first stating the thing that will be talked about, and then making a statement or asking a question about that thing (Baker & Cokely, 1980). According to Liddell (1980), indicating what is to be talked about can include first stating either the subject, the object, or the verb phrase. Researchers (Fischer, 1975; Friedman, 1976; Liddell, 1978; Baker & Cokely, 1980; and Liddell, 1980) have identified that topicalization involves the use of specific NMS - namely, raising of eyebrows accompanied by a slight tilt of the head.

It is important for the student of ASL to notice the use of NMS, the eyebrow raising and the head tilt, with the signing of the topic. Without the presence of these NMS, the following sentences are ungrammatical. The following are examples of topicalized sentences in ASL:

<u>brow raise</u>
WOMAN LIKE CAT IX
She likes this cat. **(Figure 2.1)**

<u>brow raise</u>
CAT IX   WOMAN LIKE
The woman likes this cat. **(Figure 2.2)**

<u>brow raise</u>
LIKE CAT WHO WOMAN IX
This woman likes the cat. **(Figure 2.3)**

Please refer to the DVD for:
Figure 2.1 WOMAN LIKE CAT IX
Figure 2.2 CAT IX WOMAN LIKE
Figure 2.3 LIKE CAT WHO WOMAN IX

Relative Clauses

A relative clause is a phrase that has a subject and a verb, but does not function as a complete sentence. Relative clauses, also called adjective clauses, modify nouns. In this way, relative clauses help specify to whom or what the signer is referring (Baker & Cokely, 1980: 163). Research on relative clauses in ASL (Liddell, 1978; Coulter, 1978, 1979; Liddell, 1980; Baker & Cokely, 1980) indicates that they are accompanied by specific NMS. Often, relative clauses can make use of signs such as, REMEMBER, KNOW-THAT, KNOW, and THAT (Liddell, 1980 ; Baker & Cokely, 1980). Regardless of the specific manual signs, the NMS that accompany relative clauses in ASL include raised eyebrows, and possibly a slight head tilt and upper lip raise (Liddell, 1980). The following sentences contain examples of relative clauses in ASL. The manual portion of the relative clause in figure 2.4 is "KNOW GIRL RED-HAIR THAT." The manual portion of the relative clause in figure 2.5 is "BOY RECENTLY GO."

_____ brow raise upper lip raise
KNOW GIRL RED-HAIR THAT   MY SISTER
The girl who has the red hair is my sister. **(Figure 2.4)**

_____ brow raise
BOY RECENTLY GO STEAL MONEY
The boy who just left took the money. **(Figure 2.5)**

> **Please refer to the DVD for:**
> **Figure 2.4 KNOW GIRL RED-HAIR**
> **Figure 2.5 BOY RECENTLY GO**

Once again, the use of NMS is critical to appropriately convey the intent of a relative clause. If the sentence in Figure 2.5 were signed without the NMS associated with ASL relative clauses, its meaning would be altered as follows:

BOY RECENTLY GO STEAL MONEY
The boy just went to steal some money.

Until they develop an awareness of the relevant NMS, second language learners are not only likely to incorrectly express what they intend to say, but often will misunderstand others signers.

Conditionals

Another type of sentence that is used in many languages is one that expresses a result which is based on a given condition. This sentence will include two clauses – a conditional clause and a result clause. For example, in English one might say, "If you do your homework, then you can have ice cream."

In this example, the result is that ice cream will be available, depending on one condition: whether the individual has completed the homework. In English, a conditional sentence can often be identified by the use of "if" and "then." These words are not required, however, as can be seen in this sentence: "Do your homework and you can have ice cream." In addition, the clause containing the result does not have to be a statement. This part of the sentence could just as easily be a question: "If I do my homework, can I have ice cream?"

ASL also has a structure for conditional statements, which, as in English, can take a variety of forms. It is possible to use specific signs, such as FINISH, SUPPOSE, or #IF, along with the appropriate NMS to introduce the conditional clause in ASL. Interestingly, manual signs are not necessary in such circumstances. When manual signs are not present, the only way to recognize the relationship between the two clauses as a single conditional sentence is through the use of NMS.

Research has been done (Baker & Padden, 1978; Coulter, 1978, 1979; Liddell, 1980) with regard to specific NMS used to represent conditionals. In 1986, Liddell found a unique form of NMS that is involved in ASL conditionals. The NMS associated with conditionals is comprised of raised eyebrows with the signer's head thrust outward or downward. In addition, there can be a head rotation throughout the conditional clause. The following sentence demonstrates the use of NMS in ASL conditional sentence structure:

<u>   brow raise, hd fwd   </u>   <u>   nod</u>
HOMEWORK FINISH ICE CREAM me-GIVE-you
If you finish your homework, I'll give you some ice cream.
(Figure 2.6)

> **Please refer to the DVD for:**
> **Figure 2.6 HOMEWORK FINISH**

In these types of sentences, it is only through the use of appropriate NMS that the conditional-result meaning is conveyed. In the absence of these signals, the sentence in Figure 2.6 might be an ungrammatical ASL sentence roughly translated into the ungrammatical English sentence: "The homework finished give you ice cream." Once again, it is clear that NMS play an integral role in the grammar of ASL.

Questions

In English, there are two basic types of questions people ask: polar and interrogative. Polar questions can be answered with a simple yes or no response, and are commonly referred to as yes-no questions. Interrogative questions require more detailed answers and are commonly referred to as wh-questions, since they often incorporate words such as "who," "what," "where," and so forth. ASL uses both of these types. In addition, there are special questions which are not intended to elicit a response, but merely to provide the addressee an opportunity to consider the question before the answer is supplied (Baker & Cokely, 1980). Many languages use this structure, referred to as rhetorical questions.

Research on yes-no questions in ASL (Stokoe, 1960; Fischer, 1975; Baker, 1976; Baker & Cokely, 1980; Liddell, 1980) indicates that they make use of specific NMS. These NMS include raised eyebrows with the head and/or body tilted forward. The following is an example of a yes-no question in ASL:

<u>   brow raise, hd fwd</u>
M-A-R-Y LIKE J-A-N-E?
Does Mary like Jane? **(Figure 2.7)**

> **Please refer to the DVD for:**
> **Figure 2.7 MARY LIKE JANE**

Without the use of the yes-no question NMS, the preceding sentence would most likely be construed as an assertion:

MARY LIKE JANE
Mary likes Jane.

In addition, Liddell (1980) uses the yes-no question NMS to point out that NMS must not only be present, but that they must occur at the correct time within the sentence. The NMS for yes-no questions must occur during the production of content to which the question is referring. For instance, if the raised eyebrows had only occurred during the sign LIKE, the question would not have been well-formed. Thus, it is not only important for the student of ASL to learn which

NMS represent certain grammatical aspects of ASL, but also when to apply them.

Wh-questions use NMS that are described by Baker & Cokely (1980) as a "brow squint" combined with a head tilt. These NMS can accompany a manual sign such as the sign WHAT made with two hands, palms open in front of the signer. The following is an example of a wh-question in ASL:

<u>brow squint</u>
EAT WHAT?
What are you eating?? **(Figure 2.8)**

Please refer to the DVD for:
Figure 2.8 EAT WHAT

Rhetorical questions may be accompanied by signs that normally are involved in interrogative questions, such as WHY, WHO, WHEN, WHERE, WHAT, REASON and FOR-FOR (Valli & Lucas, 1992). However, the NMS that occur with rhetorical questions are different from the NMS that occur with interrogative wh-questions. For rhetorical questions, the NMS include raised eyebrows and a small shake or tilt of the signer's head. Again, it is the NMS that make clear what type of question is being asked. An example of a rhetorical question in ASL is as follows:

<u>hd tilt/shake</u>   <u>hd shake</u>
ME HUNGRY WHY   ALL-DAY EAT NOT-YET ME
I'm really hungry because I haven't eaten anything today.
(Figure 2.9)

Please refer to the DVD for:
Figure 2.9 HUNGRY

Negation

The use of head shaking and frowning or squinting to indicate negation in ASL has been researched for many years (Stokoe, 1960; Bellugi & Fischer, 1972; Baker, 1976; Baker & Cokely, 1980; Liddell, 1980; Dively, 1996). Valli and Lucas (1992) point out that the use of NMS can be sufficient to indicate negation in a sentence. This is evidenced in the following examples:

<u>brow raise, hd tilt</u>   <u>hd shake</u>
GIRL   NOT HERE
She's not here. **(Figure 2.10)**

<u>brow raise, hd tilt</u> <u>hd shake</u>
GIRL   HERE
She isn't here. **(Figure 2.11)**

The second of these examples is dependent on the use of NMS to convey its intended meaning. The non-manual head shake is what distinguishes between the statements, "she is here" and "she isn't here." In fact, Valli & Lucas (1992) point out that a single signed utterance can have multiple meanings depending solely on the NMS that accompany the manual signs. For example, compare the meanings conveyed in figure 2.11 and figure 2.12.

<u>brow raise</u> <u>nod</u>
GIRL   HERE
She is here. **(Figure 2.12)**

Please refer to the DVD for:
Figure 2.10 - 12 GIRL HERE Sentences

NMS are necessary grammatical markers that distinguish between statements and questions in ASL. Research to date seems to indicate that the basic declarative sentence in ASL does not require NMS, but can include them. Additionally, NMS are integral to many aspects of ASL grammar, including topicalization, relative clauses, conditional statements and questions, yes-no questions, wh-questions, rhetorical questions, and negation.

This chapter has addressed various roles that NMS play in ASL grammar. The remainder of the book will focus primarily on NMS that occur on the mouth, and how these mouth morphemes modify manual signs. This focus will include descriptions of how they are produced and manual signs with which they can occur.

Chapter Two Review

1. What are grammatical markers?
2. Which facial feature often functions as a grammatical marker in ASL?
3. What does topicalization involve? What NMS are associated with this structure?
4. What is a relative clause? What NMS are associated with this structure?
5. Give an example of a conditional sentence in ASL, including appropriate NMS.
6. ASL makes use of at least three different types of questions. List these types of questions and the NMS associated with them.
7. What NMS are associated with negation in ASL?
8. Create a sentence in ASL which can have two or more different meanings depending on the NMS.

Chapter 3: Mouth Morphemes in American Sign Language

There is a great need for further studies on NMS, because there is so much information about their structure and use that has not yet been explored. There are many facial expressions used in ASL for which the linguistic meaning has not been identified. For those who are native ASL users there is a strong tendency to use non-manual signals, such as mouth morphemes, when signing. In fact, mouth morphemes are such an integral part of ASL and its structure, that when signers exclude them, their utterances are often ungrammatical or unclear. Because mouth morphemes, like the NMS discussed in the previous chapter, are an essential part of ASL, it is important to understand the concepts behind them and the roles they play.

Mouth morphemes in signed languages have been described in two ways by researchers. Some mouth morphemes seem to borrow lexical items from the local spoken language, while others do not. The former have been referred to as "mouthing" or "word pictures" (Boyes Braem, 1984; Davis, 1989; Lucas & Valli, 1989, 1992; Schermer, 1990; Vogt-Svendsen, 1984; Winston, 1989). With regard to ASL, Davis (1989) identifies various categories of mouthing that occur in ASL. He describes English mouthing as the mouthing that can accompany certain nouns, numbers, question words, fingerspelling and so forth. He describes ASL mouthing as the mouth morphemes that function as adverbs, verbs, and modals in ASL. These functions contribute to the grammar of ASL, unlike English mouthing. Davis (1989) points out that some English-like mouth movements used over long periods of time become so much a part of ASL use, and so unrecognizable as related to English, that native signers consider them a part of ASL. Along these lines, and as Johnson (1992) points out, as long as mouth movements occur as part of ASL, they should be studied as part of ASL. Thus, it is on the basis of native intuition that the mouth morphemes represented in the current materials have been selected. All of the mouth morphemes included in this chapter and the chapters that follow were judged by native signers to be ASL mouth morphemes.

ASL mouth morphemes tend to be problematic for non-native users, due to the fact that non-native signers often overlook non-manual signals. Learning NMS is easier when one knows what to look for: what certain NMS look like, and when they occur. Through informal observation it seems that of the examples of ASL mouth morphemes discussed here, appropriate use of the following is generally a good indication of native-like competency in ASL: SAO, LR-LR, CHA. If signers rarely use these mouth morphemes, chances are that they are not native users.

The use of mouth morphemes as NMS in ASL is the major focus of this chapter. Each mouth morpheme contains a wealth of information that could encompass volumes of study. For example, a single morpheme such as BOP could inspire extensive research just to examine where it occurs, how it is used, and what it means. This mouth morpheme can be used in the description of a smashed-in front fender, in the indication of something suddenly appearing or disappearing, or in describing how something was hit.

Because the examples of ASL mouth morphemes are so numerous, the purpose here is to identify these not only for students of the language, but in hope that others will be able to use this information as a basis from which to identify and classify additional mouthed NMS.

The Function of ASL Mouth Movements

ASL mouth morphemes can be used for a variety of purposes. Some mouth morphemes accompany specific signs, as in PAH which occurs with the sign FINALLY. These NMS are referred to as lexical mouth morphemes. This type of mouth morpheme is so closely linked with a given sign that in some circumstances the non-manual signal can be used without the manual sign.

ASL mouth morphemes can also function as modifiers to the manual portion of the message. When people teach signs in ASL, they do not always explain which NMS can accompany each particular sign, and how it would modify the meaning of the sign. Many signs can be modified to show various degrees of inflection. For example, the sign glossed as SMART can be inflected in a number of ways. The following chart shows a few applications along with their English equivalents:

MM SMART	Bright
OOO SMART	Clever
BRR SMART	Brilliant
SAO SMART	Genius

Verbs can also be inflected, as seen with the signs glossed as WALK and #GO. A few examples:

MM WALK	Stroll
STA-STA WALK	Walk for a long time and with great effort
TH WALK	Walk carelessly

IS #GO	Leave in a hurry
SAO #GO	Leave as quickly as possible

<u>BRR</u> #GO	**Escape (with a sense of finality)**

Figure 3.1 provides examples of mouth morpheme modifiers in use. The meaning of each utterance is modified by the use of one of three mouth morphemes: IS, OOO, and SAO.

IS

A. CAR CL:33 (pass other car) PULL-A-HAIR

OOO

B. CAR CL:33 (pass other car) PULL-A-HAIR

SAO

C. CAR CL:33 (pass other car) PULL-A-HAIR

(Figure 3.1)

> **Please refer to the DVD for:**
> **Figure 3.1 CAR SENTENCES**

These are examples of mouth morphemes being used to modify an accompanying sign, providing adverbial information. We can see parallels in in spoken languages with adverbs, word choice specificity, and stress of an utterance influencing meaning. Without the mouth morpheme, there is less clarity and detail in the signer's message.

As was discussed in the previous chapter, certain facial expressions are somewhat universal. For example, with regard to the expression that shows surprise, one would see the same kind of expressions from people with diverse linguistic backgrounds. This universality does not hold true for NMS, including mouth morphemes. For example, just as commonalities exist between Spanish and Portuguese, there are commonalities between ASL and

Italian Sign Language (LIS). Nevertheless, a signer of one cannot fully understand a signer of the other. Similarly, there appear to be some non-manual signals in LIS that are similar to non-manual signals in ASL. The function and meaning of NMS vary between signed languages and thus, unlike expressions of emotion, NMS are part of the structure of the language itself. This is another subject that needs to receive further attention from researchers.

The data for the following chapters comes primarily from an NMS research project (Bridges, 1993) conducted by the Department of ASL, Linguistics, and Interpretation at Gallaudet University. The data itself is based on native intuition, participant observations, and documentation of ASL use in a variety of real-life contexts. For each mouth morpheme that was documented, notes were made regarding the variations in production and the different situations in which these variants were used. The primary sources of the data were native ASL users interacting in various contexts all over the United States: Deaf clubs, American Athletic Association of the Deaf, deaf congregations, deaf picnics, softball tournaments, and so forth.

The collection of this data resulted in identification of more than 45 different ASL mouth morphemes. Because even the slightest differences in mouth shape or movement can evoke distinct meanings, it seems likely that there are numerous mouth morphemes not yet documented that may number well into the hundreds. One difficulty in documenting the ASL mouth morphemes was to find a way of representing them on paper. Some are represented by a gloss which reflects the action of the mouth, such as IS or OOO. Other examples were more difficult to transcribe, such as the mouth morpheme in which the tongue moves rapidly from side to side (TONGUE-HORIZON). Here we will discuss the most commonly used mouth morphemes as identified in the Bridges (1993) study.

Chapter Three Review

1. List two functions of ASL mouth morphemes.
2. How do NMS differ from seemingly universal facial expressions?

3. What is the difference between ASL mouth morphemes and English mouthing?

4. Based on the examples in this chapter, hypothesize a context in which BOP might be used.

5. With what sign does PAH occur?

6. Mouth morphemes serve many functions, one of which is providing adverbial information. To what might this be compared to in spoken language?

Chapter 4: Lexical Mouth Morphemes

So far we have addressed several types of mouth morphemes and NMS that can perform various functions. They might occur in conjunction with a variety of different signs. Some mouth morphemes, however, are linked with a specific manual sign. These mouth morphemes are included as an aspect of that sign, and are not used with any other manual sign. These are called lexical mouth morphemes.

Liddell (1980) points out that some signs are so commonly used with a specific mouth morpheme that the mouth morpheme can be used without the manual sign and still be understood. One of his examples is the sign NOT-YET, in which the tongue extends slightly, resting on the lower lip, in conjunction with the manual sign. Without the mouth morpheme, the manual sign has a different meaning: LATE. Without the manual sign, the NMS alone carries the full meaning of NOT-YET.

Lexical mouth morphemes are unlike other forms of NMS, which vary depending on the mood of the speaker or the situation in which it occurs. These NMS are linked with specific manual signs and occur either with the sign or in place of it. This chapter introduces seven lexical NMS.

Please see Chapter Four of DVD for
demonstrations and sentence examples for:
PAH
LR-LR
AF-FO
SAM
FISH
VA-VA
GA-GA-GA

PAH

PAH occurs with the sign glossed as FINALLY.

ME GRADUATE #MA <u>FINALLY</u>
I finally got my master's degree.

ME WAIT++ #BUS <u>FINALLY</u> ARRIVE
It sure took a long time for the bus to get here.

LR-LR

LR-LR occurs with the imperative (command/request) form of the sign glossed as LOOK-AT. It indicates that the addressee should follow the signer's eye gaze.

HEY <u>LOOK-AT(right)</u> TEACHER <u>LOOK-AT(right)</u>
Hey, look at the teacher over there!

T-O-M BREAK PANTS Z-I-P-P-E-R CL:BB <u>LOOK-AT(right)</u>
Tom's zipper broke - check it out!

AF-FO

AF-FO occurs with the sign glossed as HAVE-TO.

WORK ME <u>HAVE-TO</u> GO (disappointed)
Unfortunately I have to go to work.

BOSS boss-TELL-me TOMORROW ME WORK <u>HAVE-TO</u>
(disappointed)
My supervisor says I've got to work tomorrow.

SAM

SAM occurs with the sign glossed as SAME.

> REALLY <u>SAME-ME</u> TEST D-GRADE <u>SAME-ME</u>!
> *Wow, I can't believe we both got a D on the exam!*

> YOU WORK #PO? <u>SAME-ME</u>
> *You work at the Post Office? So do I!*

FISH

FISH (also written as FSH) occurs with the sign glossed as FINISH.

> TEST ME *FINISH* (relived)
> *I'm finally done with the exam.*

> STUDY++ TEST <u>FINISH</u> ME
> *I spent a lot of time preparing for that test.*

VA-VA

VA-VA (or VA) occurs with the sign glossed as HAVE.

> M-A-C COMPUTER C-A-S-S <u>HAVE++</u>
> *Cass has a Macintosh.*

> MOVIE TICKET <u>HAVE++</u> YOU?
> *Did you get a ticket for the movie yet?*

GA-GA-GA

GA-GA-GA occurs with the sign glossed as DRINK (verb).

EXERCISE FINISH ME TEND <u>DRINK</u> WATER
I always chug a glass of water after a workout.

FEEL GOOD WATER <u>DRINK</u> (satisfied)
That water really hit the spot.

Chapter Four Review

Identify the lexical mouth morpheme that would occur in each of the following ASL sentences.

1. SPORT TICKET HAVE YOU
2. PROJECT ME FINISH
3. YOU WORK #BANK SAME-ME?
4. WOW FAST DRINK YOU
5. HEY LOOK-AT MOON LOOK-AT
6. MY MOM HAVE MAC COMPUTER
7. M-A-R-I-A NEW CAR LOOK-AT
8. ME WAIT++ FINALLY SHOW START
9. RUN FINISH ME TEND WATER DRINK
10. SORRY ME HAVE-TO LEAVE HAVE-TO
11. ME TRY++ FAIL SAME
12. MOM she-INFORM-me HAVE-TO SCHOOL TOMORROW
13. SILLY FINISH
14. SON LICENSE FINALLY

Deaf <u>Tend</u> Your

Chapter 5: Mouth Morpheme Modifiers

NMS are often used in ASL to modify manual signs. As early as 1976, Baker writes about the use of puffed cheeks and widened eyes to modify the sign TREE to include information about its size. Further research on the use of NMS as modifiers, including closed eyes, wrinkled nose, and so forth, can be found in the work of Liddell (1977, 1980), Baker & Padden (1978), Coulter (1978, 1979), and Baker & Cokely (1980). Liddell (1977) identifies specific NMS which are used as adverbs in ASL. In addition, an extensive description of NMS modifiers exists in Baker & Cokely's (1980) work. The following are examples of mouth morphemes which modify ASL manual signs.

> **Please see Chapter Five of DVD for**
> **demonstrations and sentence examples for:**
> **MM**
> **CS**
> **TH**
> **Puffed Cheek**
> **Intense**
> **Pursed Lips**
> **STA-STA**
> **ZZ**
> **IS**
> **BRR**
> **SAO**
> **CHA**
> **UR**

MM

MM indicates the action is done in an ordinary manner. MM can occur with many verbs including DRIVE, LOOK, SHOP, GO-STEADY, and WRITE. It is also used in lieu of a manual verb to express the concept "to be at."

ME <u>DRIVE</u>
I was driving.

ME <u>ENJOY STUDY</u>
I like to study.

CS

CS indicates the object or action is close in space or time. CS can occur with such signs as RECENTLY, CLOSE-TO, ARRIVE, NOW, and NEXT-TO.

<u>RECENTLY</u> TEST ME FINISH
I just finished my exam.

YOUR HOME <u>ACROSS</u>
It's across the street from your house.

TH

TH indicates the action is done in a careless manner. It is also used in lieu of a manual verb to express information about state of being. TH can occur with a variety of signs such as COMMENT and DRIVE.

ME <u>SHOP++</u>
I shopped absentmindedly.

Puffed cheeks

Puffed Cheeks indicate magnitude, which can include large size or quantity.

OUTSIDE RAIN++ <u>AWFUL</u>
It's raining cats and dogs out there.

ME ACCIDENT AWFUL <u>FUNNY-ZERO</u>
I was in a serious accident.

Intense

Intense indicates extreme emphasis.

B-E-A-C-H WOW PEOPLE <u>CL:55</u> MANY!
The beach was packed!

Pursed Lips

Pursed Lips indicate enjoyment, ease, or small/thin/smooth objects.

KNOW N-A-S-C-A-R ME <u>KISS-FIST (nod)</u>!
NASCAR is awesome!

MOTORCYCLE ME LIKE <u>DRIVE-MOTORCYCLE (nod)</u>
I love riding motorcycles.

STA-STA

STA-STA indicates the action happens for an unusually long time, or with great intensity. STA-STA can be used to inflect signs such as WORK, STAND, STUDY, TYPE, FINGERSPELL, PRACTICE, READ, CLEAN, WALK, WRITE, and WAIT.

LAST NIGHT ME AWAKE ALL-NIGHT WHY? <u>STUDY</u>++
I pulled an all-nighter studying last night.

ME <u>STRUGGLE</u>++ MECHANIC-WORK FINALLY MOTOR-RUN
I worked on the engine until I finally got it going.

IS

IS indicates a high level of intensity. It can occur with such signs as BARELY, AWFUL, RIDICULOUS, CLOSE, SMART, DANCE, FINGERSPELL, PRACTICE, READ, WANT, CHEAP, CLEAN, DIRTY, EXPENSIVE, EXPLAIN, and SORRY. It is used similarly to ZZ.

YOU <u>LUCKY</u> YOU
You lucky dog you.

UNBELIEVABLE <u>PULL-A-HAIR</u> COP ALMOST CATCH-me
I narrowly escaped the cops!

ZZ

ZZ indicates a high level of intensity. It is used similarly to IS, and can occur with such signs as SPEEDING and SORRY.

ME <u>HURRY++</u> WORK
I have to hurry and get to work.

COP CATCH-me WHY? ME <u>SPEED</u>
I got pulled over for speeding.

BRR

BRR indicates intensity (including size and quantity), indifference, or onomatopoeic attributes. It can occur with such signs as, CL:55 (many people), CL:bentLL (shooting machine gun), BORED, COLD, BEAUTIFUL, SMART, STUPID, GOOD-FRIEND, FINGERSPELL, AWFUL, CHEAP, DIRTY, EXPENSIVE, and FEELING.

IX B-E-A-C-H UNBELIEVABLE PEOPLE <u>CL:55</u>
The beach was crowded.

REALLY ME SICK-OF MAN <u>BOTHER++</u>
I've had it with that guy bugging me.

SAO

SAO (also written as SOA or SOW) indicates extreme emphasis. It can occur with signs such as SICK-OF, HATE, SMART, CHEAP, EXPENSIVE, PROUD, FULL, and LUCKY.

REALLY ME <u>SICK-OF</u> LOOK-ME++
I'm fed up with being stared at!

UNBELIEVABLE ME <u>FULL</u>
Man, am I stuffed!

CHA

CHA indicates the object is large and/or thick.

UNBELIEVABLE B-O-B HOME <u>CL:claw</u>
Bob's house is gigantic!

P-I-Z-Z-A ME LIKE <u>CL:openG</u>
I like thick-crust pizza.

UR

UR indicates the action is done in a careless or foolish manner, and is used similarly to TH. It can be associated with mindless activities that could be dangerous. Commonly used when mocking other's actions.

THINK ME <u>PITY-you?</u> NO-NO
I'm not going to feel sorry for you.

H-A-R-R-Y <u>TALK-TO-SELF</u> AWFUL
Harry talks to himself - can you believe it?

Chapter Five Review

The following sentences can each be produced with several different mouth morpheme modifiers. Create as many options as you can for each sentence using the modifiers found in this chapter.

1. ME BUY BOOK CL:C
2. ME SEE DRUNK MAN CL:1
3. YOUR HOME CLOSE
4. WOMAN BATHROOM CL:44 MANY
5. MAN POUR KNOW C-O-N-C-R-E-T-E CL:BB
    WOW SMOOTH CL:BB
6. MOM SMART
7. ME LITTLE-BIT EXERCISE
8. PRICE CHEAP
9. RECENTLY ME FINISH TEST
10. STORE ME GO CASUAL LOOK
11. WARN IMPORTANT REMEMBER
12. ME CATCH BIG FISH
13. ME PRACTICE++ FINGERSPELL
14. W-I-N-K PERFORM MANY PEOPLE CL:55

Deaf <u>Tend</u> Your

Thus far, the mouth morphemes we've looked at have fit into distinct categories. This chapter will cover mouth morphemes that are not as easily categorized. These morphemes serve various roles in ASL, and will be discussed individually, with many appearing in a range of contexts.

Several of the mouth morphemes we've covered so far have had onomatopoeic attributes, such as BRR and GA-GA-GA. A number of them have had possible English roots, such as FA and WA. These etymological speculations suggest a topic that warrants further investigation. Some of the mouth morphemes found in Chapter 6 and 7 will also exhibit these features.

> **Please see Chapter Six of DVD for demonstrations and sentence examples for:**
> **WHOP**
> **BA-BA-BA**
> **POW**
> **AAH**
> **OOO**
> **OOOA**
> **PO**
> **EEE**
> **BOP**
> **BE-BE-BE**
> **PEY**
> **AB**
> **TONGUE-HORIZON**
> **FFF**

WHOP

WHOP indicates emphasis. It can be used with signs such as BIGHEAD and BORED.

REALLY++ YOU <u>BIGHEAD</u> YOU
You're really arrogant, aren't you.

MY TEAM BASKETBALL <u>BLOW-OUT</u> OTHER TEAM.
We crushed the other team in basketball.

BA-BA-BA

BA-BA-BA indicates non-specific speech acts, and/or influence from spoken English (English root). It is used with signs such as BAD, BUT, TELL and TALK.

IX TEND <u>TALK-ON-PHONE</u>++
They're always gabbing on the phone.

IX TEND <u>BEG</u>++ PEOPLE
He's such a mooch.

POW

POW indicates unexpectedness, frustration and/or anger, or onomatopoeic attributes. It often occurs in situations such as accidents, getting sick, and winning large prizes.

KNOW L-O-T-T-E-R-Y LAST-WEEK ME <u>HIT</u> 500 DOLLAR
I won $500 in the lottery last week!

ME SICK <u>LAID-UP</u> BAD WOW
I was sick as a dog.

AAH

AAH indicates far distance, feelings of awe/engagement, or an extended period of time. It can be used with signs such as SORRY, ALL-DAY, ALL-NIGHT.

KNOW LINCOLN L-I-N-C-O-L-N S-T-A-T-U-E ME <u>LOOK-UP</u>
The Lincoln Memorial is awe-inspiring!

THINK ME WALK <u>FAR-AWAY?</u> (indigent)
There's no way I'm walking that far.

OOO

OOO indicates smallness, emotional realization, or extremeness. It can be used with signs such as THIN, WOW, NEAT, NEW, AWFUL, OH-I-SEE, LONG-AGO.

<u>AWFUL</u>
That's terrible!

<u>WOW</u> EXPERT YOU
Hey, you're good!

OOOA

OOOA indicates smallness, emotional realization, or extremeness. It is used similarly to OOO, and can occur with such signs as THIN, COOL, WOW, AWFUL, and YOUNG.

OUTSIDE FINE-wg <u>COOL</u>
It's nice and cool outside.

RIGHT++ GIRL <u>YOUNG</u>
Yeah, it's because she's young.

PO

PO indicates small sizes.

> ME THINK CL:claw FIND <u>CL:claw</u> SICK-OF YOU
> *You made me think this would be much larger!*

> FOOD ME IMAGINE CL:claw FIND <u>CL:claw</u> (disappointed)
> *I was disappointed by the small servings.*

EEE

EEE indicates lacking, frustration, intense emotions, or onomatopoeic attributes.

> WAVE HEARING-AID <u>SQUEAL</u> IX
> *Your hearing aid is making noise.*

> <u>SORRY</u>
> *I'm really sorry.*

BOP

BOP indicates rapid action or onomatopoeic attributes.

> ME PLAN++ <u>MESS-UP </u>FINISH
> *Now all my plans are ruined.*

> S-T-E-V-E HAPPEN? <u>DISAPPEAR</u>
> *Steve's nowhere to be found - what's up?*

BE-BE-BE

BE-BE-BE indicates a sense of judgement, anger, or contempt, and often accompanies a non-specific speech act. It is used with signs such as BRAG, COMMENT, LOOK-UP-DOWN, GROUCHY.

ME <u>BOIL</u> WHY? BEFORE STEAL MY MONEY
I'm livid about my money being stolen!

CAREFUL IX TEND <u>GOSSIP</u> CAREFUL
Heads up - that one can't keep a secret.

PEY
PEY indicates a sense of emphasis, consistency, or singularity. It is often used with signs such as TEND, PRINT, HEADLINE, GET-TICKET, THRILL, and PENNY.

IX TALK++ MAKE-UP++ OFF-POINT++ <u>TEND</u> IX
I can never follow his random tangents.

K-A-T-H-Y <u>TEND</u> OFF-POINT++
Kathy is all over the place.

AB

AB indicates a sense of closure, either literal or metaphorical. It is used with signs such as STAY, QUIET, MOUTH-SHUT, ACCEPT, and GET-UP.

YOU NOT TELL-them YOU <u>MOUTH-SHUT</u> YOU
Don't tell a living soul.

NOW TIME <u>GET-UP</u>
It's time to get up!

TONGUE-HORIZON

TONGUE-HORIZON indicates elaboration or excitement. It is often used with signs such as FINE-wg, IX-FAR, and WANT.

<u>FINE-wg</u> ICE-CREAM ME HAVE YOU NONE (nod)
Ha, ha! I have an ice cream cone and you don't!

ME <u>WANT</u> WHAT? CHOCOLATE ICE-CREAM ME WANT
ME
<u>*I really want some chocolate ice cream!*</u>

FFF

FFF indicates emphasis and/or influence from spoken English (English root). It is used with signs such as SORRY, AWFUL, REALLY, FUNNY, SHAME-ON-YOU, and KNIFE.

REALLY++ ME <u>PITY</u> J-O-H-N
I feel so sorry for John.

<u>AWFUL</u>
Oh, that's terrible!

Chapter Six Review

The following sentences can each be produced with several different mouth morphemes. Create as many options as you can for each sentence using the mouth morphemes found in this chapter.

1. SHOW WATCH BORING
2. ME WRITE ENGLISH CAN BUT HE BETTER
3. DOCTOR TELL ME J-O-H-N BAD HEART MUST OPERATE
4. CAR WALL BAD HIT
5. HAPPEN HIT LARGE MONEY GIVE-me
6. ME WORK ALL-DAY
7. ME DRIVE FAR-AWAY
8. LONG-AGO
9. WOW NEAT
10. PHONE NEW THIN
11. GROUP ALL YOUNG
12. MY NEW CAR SMALL
13. MACHINE SQUEAL HEAR CAN
14. WOW SORRY
15. CAR FAST DISAPPEAR
16. ME TAKE-OFF-FAST
17. P-E-T-E-R C-O-O-K FUNNY!
18. SHAME-ON IX
19. YES TEND HAPPEN
20. ME TELL YOU ACCEPT
21. STOP QUIET
22. DISNEY-WORLD ME GO WANT

Deaf Tend Your

**Please see Chapter Seven of DVD for
demonstrations and sentence examples for:**
FA++
BA
BEY
FOMP
FA
WA
AS
SA
MA
BAO
SHHH
LUP
BAH
PU

BA

BA indicates influence from spoken English (English root).

> ME WRITE ENGLISH CAN <u>BUT</u> IX BETTER IX
> *I can write English but he's better at it than I am.*

> DOCTOR TELL-me J-O-H-N HEART <u>BAD</u> MUST OPERATE
> *The doctor says John needs heart surgery.*

FA++

FA++ indicates influence from spoken English (English root). occurring with each repeated sign.

> MOTHER IX FATHER IX TWO-OF-THEM <u>ARGUE</u>
> *Mom and dad are always at each other's throats.*

> MONEY FATHER <u>FIND++</u>
> *My dad keeps finding money all over the place.*

BEY

BEY indicates a sense of emphasis. It is used with signs such as PRINT, BIG-WORD, and SAME.

> HEY SEE ME <u>PRINT CL:G</u> (pose) PICTURE?
> *Did you see my picture in the paper?*

> MAN INVEST S-T-O-C-K <u>HIT</u> RICH UNBELIEVABLE
> *He made it big in the stock market.*

FOMP

FOMP indicates a sense of dismissal, lack of caring, or abandonment of responsibility.

ME GO-OUT NEW-YORK C-I-T-Y NONE MONEY <u>SO-WHAT</u>
Being broke won't stop me from going to New York!

TEST TOMORROW ME STUDY <u>NAH</u>
I'm not gonna study for tomorrow's test.

FA

FA indicates influence from spoken English (English root).

GIVE-me #TV? <u>FINE++</u>
Sure, you can give me your TV.

ME LOOK-AT++ #TV LAST NIGHT REALLY++ <u>FUNNY</u>
UNBELIEVABLE
I saw a hilarious TV show last night.

WA

WA sometimes indicates onomatopoeic attributes or influence from spoken English (English root). Other instances of WA require further research to be fully understood. WA is used with signs such as WANT, WHAT, WHY, WATER, RAIN, and RUN.

OUTSIDE <u>RAIN++</u> AWFUL
It's raining cats and dogs out there.

ME QUIT WORK <u>WHY?</u> INCREASE BOSS NO-me
My boss wouldn't give me a raise, so I quit.

AS

AS sometimes indicates onomatopoeic attributes or influence from spoken English (English root). Other instances of AS require further research to be fully understood. AS is used with signs such as ASK, REQUEST, UNTIL, IDEA, and ACCIDENT.

ME <u>ACCIDENT</u> AWFUL FUNNY-ZERO
I was in a serious accident.

LITTLE GIRL DOG <u>BITE</u>-arm
A dog attacked the little girl.

SA

SA sometimes indicates onomatopoeic attributes or influence from spoken English (English root). Other instances of SA require further research to be fully understood. SA is used with signs such as SHOCK, SAD, DON'T-KNOW, SORRY, and CRY.

SOMEONE TELL-ME, ME <u>SHOCK</u> ME
I can't believe what I just found out!

ME <u>SAD</u> WHY? YOUR CAT DIE
I was sad to hear your cat passed away.

MA

MA sometimes indicates onomatopoeic attributes or influence from spoken English (English root). Other instances of MA require further research to be fully understood.

BOY <u>MAD</u> WHY? SOMEONE STOLE HIS BIKE
He's upset that his bike was stolen.

CAR NOT YOUR, <u>MY</u>
That's my car, not yours.

BAO

BAO indicates onomatopoeic attributes (also written as BOA or BOW).

HAPPEN ROCKET <u>BOOM</u>
The rocket took off and exploded.

SHHH

SHHH sometimes indicates onomatopoeic attributes. Other instances of SHHH require further research to be fully understood. SHHH is used with signs such as SHOWER, SPRAY, HUSH, MISCHIEVOUS, and SPEED.

PLEASE <u>HUSH</u> NOT TELL K-A-T-H-Y
Please don't tell Kathy.

YESTERDAY DO-DO? <u>PAINT-THE-TOWN</u>
Yesterday we went out on the town.

LUP

LUP sometimes indicates the disappearance of an entity. Other instances of LUP require further research to be fully understood. LUP is used with signs such as BORED, WHIP-OTHER-TEAM, and DISAPPEAR.

ME <u>OVER-IT</u> KNOW TRAVEL++ SEE++
I've seen all there is to see of the world.

KNOW D-A-L-L-A-S COWBOY FOR-SURE <u>BLOW-OUT</u>
EAGLE
You know the Dallas Cowboys are gonna kill the Eagles.

BAH

BAH is made with an intake of breath and can indicate capitulation. Other instances of BAH require further research to be fully understood. BAH is used with signs such as GIVE-IN and GIVE-TO.

ME <u>GIVE-IN</u> JOIN GO-OUT NEW-YORK C-I-T-Y
I reluctantly decided to go with them to New York.

J-O-H-N JOIN MY HOME SLEEP ME *GIVE-IN*
<u>I went ahead and let John stay with me.</u>

PU

PU can indicate emphasis. Other instances of PU require further research to be fully understood. PU is used with signs such as SHOOT, ONE-UP, PERFECT, and BEAT.

RACE CAR ME <u>BEAT</u>
My car could outdo yours any day.

WHAT HAPPEN HE <u>BEAT</u> YOU
How come he beat you?

Chapter Seven Review

The following sentences can each be produced with several different mouth morphemes. Create as many options as you can for each sentence using the mouth morphemes found in this chapter.

1. ME BAD DAY
2. ME FIGHT++ ALMOST 3 YEAR
3. HOPE NEW, NO SAME
4. IX BRAG, NAH
5. ME FIND YOU
6. WHAT?!
7. ME REQUEST IX, NO-me
8. #WOW ME DON'T-KNOW
9. ME ENJOY SHOWER, FEEL GOOD
10. SEE CAR EXPLODE
11. ME SIMPLE ASK, IX MAD
12. READ++ BORED
13. GIVE-IN FINE COME-ON
14. ALMOST PERFECT!
15. RESEARCH FIND++
16. NO CAN'T BUT TOMORROW CAN
17. C-R-O-M FUNNY!
18. DRIVE FAR SO-WHAT
19. READ SEE BIG-WORD
20. IX TV WANT?
21. ME IDEA WRITE-DOWN
22. ME CRY++
23. ME MISCHIEVOUS TEND
24. B-O-B DISAPPEAR, HAPPEN?
25. TEACHER EASY ONE-UP

Chapter 8: The Importance of Non-Manual Signals in ASL

Learning ASL mouth morphemes is an interesting and time-consuming process. Chapter One discussed the importance of NMS and addressed facial expressions as expressing emotional states, constructed action, and conversation regulators; Chapter Two focused on NMS as grammatical markers; Chapter Three described the procedures used to collect information about the NMS mouth morphemes included in this book, and began to focus specifically on ASL mouth morphemes; Chapter Four discusses lexicalized mouth morphemes; mouth morpheme modifiers are shown in Chapter Five. Additional mouth morphemes are covered in Chapter Six and Seven. This chapter will review the information discussed throughout this book.

ASL mouth morphemes are a meaningful aspect of ASL that do not require the use of the hands. Thus, they are a form of non-manual signal, or NMS. In ASL, NMS can involve the use of the mouth, cheeks, eyes, and/or eyebrows in various facial expressions. In addition, they can include head and/or body movements. Future research on NMS will undoubtedly reveal further information about these movements and expressions.

NMS can function in a variety of ways: grammatical markers, integral parts of lexical signs, conversation regulators, constructed action, and as universal expressions of emotion. They can also function in a way that can be described as similar to vocal intonation in spoken languages.

Some facial expressions reflecting the emotions of a signer are universal signals, rather than being associated specifically with ASL. In other words, when a signer's face shows feelings of sadness or happiness, the same facial expressions would be used to reflect these feelings in a large number of the world's cultures, regardless of language. Of course, the cause and timing of these facial expressions may vary from culture to culture. Nevertheless, the facial expressions of the signer are meaningful to the act of communicating, though they are not a purely linguistic act.

Another common occurrence of NMS is within constructed action. Constructed action refers to the parts of an utterance in which the signer actually demonstrates a character's actions. For instance, when a signer mentions someone looking around for possible observers, the signer may look around without signing anything manually. This is a form of constructed action; the signer is recreating the actions they are talking about. Constructing the actions of characters involves the use of non-manual signals.

NMS can be used to help regulate turn taking in a given conversation. Frequently, eye gaze functions as a conversation regulator in ASL. A signer will often make eye contact to begin their turn in a conversation, but need not maintain it throughout their turn. Reestablishing eye contact is then a way to indicate the turn is completed, allowing another to take a turn. Conversation regulators can function in a variety of ways depending on the setting. Recall that a teacher might use various eye gaze techniques to maintain control of a class discussion in ASL.

Mouth morphemes also can occur with a manual sign. Lexical mouth morphemes tend to occur with a specific sign, and sometimes can be substituted for that sign. One example of this is the sign for NOT-YET which involves the tongue protruding through the lips slightly and means "not yet" even when made without the accompanying manual sign. Another example of a lexical mouth morpheme is PAH, which occurs with the manual sign FINALLY.

The use of NMS as grammatical markers has received a great deal of attention. NMS function as grammatical markers in many ASL structures including relative clauses, conditional clauses, yes-no questions, wh-questions, rhetorical questions, topicalization, and negation. To demonstrate the impact of NMS as grammatical markers, consider the possible meanings communicated by the following sentence. Note that the meanings are dependent upon NMS to convey the intent of the signer:

WOMAN KISS-FIST FOOTBALL
The woman loves football.

When this utterance is accompanied by NMS, the meaning and function of the phrase can be clarified. When the eyebrows are raised during the first sign, for example, the subject has become a topic and the rest of the sentence functions as a comment:

<u>brows raise</u>
WOMAN   KISS-FIST FOOTBALL
She loves football

If the brows are raised, the head is tilted slightly, and the upper lip is raised throughout the utterance, it functions as a relative clause. Not only does the phrase become descriptive of someone supposedly familiar, but these three signs are now an incomplete sentence which appear to be ungrammatical unless followed by additional information.

<u>   brow raise, hd tilt, lip raise</u>
WOMAN KISS-FIST FOOTBALL...
The woman who loves football...

The use of raised eyebrows combined with a head thrust on the last of the three signs indicates that the phrase is now the condition upon which some outcome must rest. For instance, the signer might be saying, "If she loves football, then invite her to the game." Again, the three signs accompanied by these NMS are not a complete sentence and are ungrammatical if left standing alone.

<u>   brow raise, hd thrust</u>
WOMAN KISS-FIST FOOTBALL...
If she loves football, then...

When these three signs are produced with the eyebrows raised and the head tilted forward, they represent a yes-no question. In this case, the three signs can stand alone as a completely grammatical sentence.

hd fwd, brow raise

WOMAN KISS-FIST FOOTBALL
Does she like football?

Finally, the last example is a negative statement that the woman does not like football. The only way to determine that this particular sentence is not affirmative is through the non-manual head shake. This sentence is grammatical without requiring further input from the signer.

hd shake

WOMAN KISS-FIST FOOTBALL
She doesn't like football.

Clearly, the impact of NMS is significant when functioning as grammatical markers in ASL. It seems obvious why people who learn ASL as a second language and are unaware of NMS in ASL can experience many frustrations and misunderstandings. Because NMS are such an integral part of ASL, it is essential that they are recognized and used correctly.

The information contained in this book is intended to assist in the understanding of NMS in ASL. Students of ASL, native ASL users studying the language, teachers, interpreters, and those working in bilingual-bicultural programs can study NMS to improve their ASL competence. In addition, they should make use of the diverse research done in the field of ASL linguistics, dating back to the early work of William Stokoe in the 1960s. As technology continues to improve, Deaf and hearing people are likely to have increased opportunities to communicate visually.

Dr. Byron Bridges and Dr. Melanie Metzger

Appendix

Chapter 3
SAO/SOA/SOW
LR-LR
CHA
BOP
IS
OOO

Chapter 4
PAH
LR-LR
AF-FO
SAM
FISH
VA-VA
GA-GA-GA

Chapter 5
MM
CS
TH
Puffed Cheeks
Intense
Pursed Lips
STA-STA
IS
ZZ
BRR
SAO/SOA/SOW
CHA
UR

Chapter 6
WHOP

BA-BA-BA
POW
AAH
OOO
OOOA
PO
EEE
BOP
BE-BE-BE
PEY
AB
TONGUE-HORIZON
FFF

Chapter 7
BA
FA++
BEY
FOMP
FA
WA
AS
SA
MA
BAO/BOA/BOW
SHHH
LUP
BAH
PU

Dr. Byron Bridges and Dr. Melanie Metzger

References

Baker, C. 1976. Eye-openers in ASL. Sixth Annual California Linguistics Association Conference: Proceedings. 1-13.

Baker, C. 1976. What's not on the other hand in American Sign Language. In S. Hufwene, C.Walker, and S. Streeven (eds) Papers from the 12th Regional Meeting of the Chicago Linguistics Society. Chicago, Illinois.

Baker, C. 1977. Regulators and turn-taking in American Sign Language discourse. In L. Friedman (ed) On the Other Hand: New Perspectives on American Sign Language. New York: Academic Press. 215-236.

Baker, C. and D. Cokely. 1980. American Sign Language: A teacher's resource text on grammar and culture. Silver Springs, MD: T.J. Publishers, Inc.

Baker, C. and C. Padden. 1978. Focusing on the non-manual components of American Sign Language. In P. Siple (ed) Understanding Language Through Sign Language Research. New York: Academic Press. 59-90.

Bellugi, U. and S. Fischer. 1972. A comparison of sign language and spoken language: Rate and grammatical mechanisms. Cognition: International Journal of Cognitive Psychology. 1. 173-200.

Boyes Braem, P. 1984. Studying Swiss German sign dialects. In Lonckectal (ed) Recent Research on European Sign Languages. Liss, Swetz and Zeitlinger.

Bridges, B. 1993. Non-manual signals in ASL. Unpublished manuscript. Washington, D.C.: Gallaudet University.

Bridges, B. 1993. Perspective shift in ASL. Unpublished manuscript. Washington, D.C.: Gallaudet University.

Coulter, G. 1978. Raised eyebrows and wrinkled noses: The functions of facial expression in relative clauses and related constructions. In Caccamise (ed) Proceedings of the Second National Symposium on Sign Language Research and Teaching. Silver Spring, MD: National Association of the Deaf.

Coulter, G. 1979. American Sign Language Typology. Ph. dissertation. University of California, San Diego.

Davis. J. 1989. Distinguishing language contact phenomena in ASL interpretation. In C. Lucus (ed) The sociolinguistics of the Deaf Community. San Diego, CA: Academic Press. 85-102.

Dively, V. 1996. Native Deaf people in the U.S. and American Sign Language: Nonhand signs. PHD Dissertation. Union Insitute Graduate School Cincinnati, Ohio.

Ekman, P. and W. Friesen. 1975. Unmasking the face. Englewood Cliffs, NJ: Prentice Hall.

Engberg-pedersen, E. 1992. Speech reports, reported thoughts, and other kinds of reports. Paper presented to the Fourth International Conference on Theoretical Issues in Sign Language Research. San Diego, CA.

Fisher, S. 1975. Influences on word order change in American Sign Language. In C. Li (ed) Word Order and Word Order Change. Austin, TX: University of Texas Press. 1-25

Friedman, L. 1975. Space, time, and person reference in American Sign Language. Language. 51. 950-961.

Friedman, L. 1976. The manifestation of subject, object, and topic in American Sign Language. In C. Li (ed) Subject and Topic. Austin. TX: University of Texas Press. 125-148

Johnson, R.E. 1992. Possible Infulences on bilingualism in early ASL acquisition. Paper presented to the Fourth International Conference on Theoretical Issues in Sign Language Research. San Diego, CA

Kendon, A. 1988. How gestures can become like words. In F. Poyatos (ed) Cross-cultural Perspectives in Nonverbal Communication. Toronto: Hogrefe. 131-141.

Klima, E. and U. Bellugi. 1979. The signs of language. Cambridge, MA: Hardvard University Press.

Kegl, J. and R. Wilbur, 1976. When does structure stop and style begin? Syntax, morphology and phonology vs. stylistic variations in American Sign Language. In S. Hufwene, C. Walker, and S. Streevens (eds). Papers from the 12th Regional Meeting of the Chicago Linguistic Society. Chicago, Illinois

Lentz, E. M. 1986. Teaching role shifting. In C. Padden (ed) Proceedings of the Fourth National Symposium on Sign Language Research and Teaching. Silver Spring, MD: National Association of the Deaf. 58-59.

Liddell, S. 1977. An investigation into the syntactic structure of American Sign Language. Ph.D. dissertation. University of California, San Diego.

Liddell, S. 1978. Non-manual signals and relative clauses in American Sign Language. In P. Siple (ed) Understanding Language Through Sign Language Research. New York: Academic Press. 59–90.

Liddell, S. 1980. American Sign Language syntax. The Hague: Mouton.

Liddell, S. 1986. Head thrust in ASL conditional marking. Sign Language Studies. 52. 243–262.

Liddell, S. 1995. Real, surrogate, and token space: Grammatical consequences in ASL. In K. Emmoery and J. Reilly (eds) language, Gesture, and space. Hillsdale, New Jersey: Lawrence Erlbaum Associates. 19–41.

Liddell, S. (in press) Tokens and surrogates. In I. Ahlgren, B. Bergman, and M. Brennan. (ed) Proceedings of the Fifth International Conference on Sign Language Research. Salamanca, Spain.

Liddell, S. and R. E. Johnson. 1989. American Sign Language: The phonological base. Sign Language Studies. 64. 195–277.

Lucas, C. and C. Valli. 1989. Language contact in the American deaf community. In C.

Lucas (ed) The sociolinguistics of the Deaf Community. San Diego, CA: Academic Press. 11–40.

_____. 1991. ASL or contact signing: Issues of judgment. Language in Society. 20. 201–216.

_____. 1992. Language contact in the American Deaf community. San Diego, CA: Academic Press.

Mather, S. 1989. Visually oriented teaching strategies. In C. Lucas (ed) The Sociolinguistics of the Deaf community. San Diego, CA: Academic Press. 165–187.

McNeill, D. 1992. Hand and mind: What gestures reveal about thought. Chicago, IL: University of Chicago Press.

Metzger, M. 1995. Constructed dialogue and constructed action in American Sign Language. In C. Lucas (ed) The Sociolinguistics of the Deaf community. Washington, D.C.: Gallaudet University Press 255–271.

Padden, C. 1986. Verbs and role-shifting in American Sign Language. In C. Padden (ed) Proceedings of the Fourth International Symposium on Sign Language Research and Teaching. Silver Springs, M.D.: National Association of the Deaf. 44–57.

Roy, C. 1989. Features of discourse in an American sign language lecture. In C.

Lucas (ed) The sociolinguistics of the Deaf Community. San Diego, CA: Academic Press. 231-251.

Schermer, T.M. 1990. In search of a language. Influence from spoken Dutch on the sign Language of the Netherlands. Delft. Eburon.

Stokoe, W. 1960. Sign language structure: an outline of the visual communication system of the American Deaf. Studies in Linguistics, Occasional Papers, Vol. 8. Buffalo, NY: University of Buffalo (revise 1978. Silver Spring, MD: Linstok Press.)

Stokoe, W. D. Casterline, and C. Croneberg. 1965. A dictionary of American Sign Language on linguistic principles. Silver Spring, MD: Linstok Press.

Valli, C. and C. Lucas. 1992. Linguistics of American sign language: A resource texts for ASL users. Washington, D.C: Gallaudet University Press.

Vogt-Svendsen, M. 1984. Word pictures in Norwegian Sign Language – A preliminary analysis. Working papers in linguistics. 2. Trondheim: University of Trondheim.

Winston, Elizabeth. 1989. Transliteration: What's the message. In C. Lucas (ed) The sociolinguistics of the Deaf Community. San Diego, CA: Academic Press. 147-164.

Winston, Elizabeth. 1991. Spatial referencing and cohesion in American Sign Language text. Sign Language Studies. 73. 397–410.

Winston, Elizabeth. 1992. Space and involvement in an American Sign Language lecture. In J. Plant - Moeller (ed) Expanding Horizons: Proceedings of the Twelfth National Convention of the Registry of Interpreters for the Deaf. Silver Spring, MD: RID Publications. 93-105.